SAVING WILDLIFE

Sally Morgan

FRANKLIN WATTS
LONDON • SYDNEY

First published in 2007 by
Franklin Watts
338 Euston Road, London NW1 3BH

Franklin Watts Australia
Level 17/207 Kent Street, Sydney, NSW 2000

EARTH SOS is based on the series Earth Watch published by Franklin Watts. It was produced for Franklin Watts by Bender Richardson White, P O Box 266, Uxbridge UB9 5NX.
Project Editor: Lionel Bender
Text Editor: Jenny Vaughan
Original text adapted and updated by: Jenny Vaughan
Designer: Ben White
Picture Researchers: Cathy Stastny and Daniela Marceddu
Media Conversion and Make-up: Mike Weintroub,MW Graphics, and Clare Oliver
Cover Design and Make-up: Mike Pilley, Pelican Graphics
Production Kim Richardson

For Franklin Watts:
Series Editor: Melanie Palmer
Art Director: Jonathan Hair
Cover design: Chi Leung

A CIP catalogue record for this book is available from the British Library.

Dewey classification 591.68
ISBN 978 0 7496 7674 2
Printed in China

Picture Credits Tony Stone Image: cover main image (Manoi Shah) and pages 5 bottom (Art Wolfe), 14-15 (Jett Britnell), 17 bottom (David Woodfall), 27 top (Manoi Shah). Oxford Scientific Films: cover small photo (Kjell Sandved) & pages 13 top (Konrad Wothe), 17 top (Colin Milkins), 18 (John McCammon), 19 (John Downer), 20 (Michael Leach), 29 bottom (Mark Hamblin). NHPA: pages 7 (Nigel J. Dennis), 9 bottom (Haroldo Palo Jr.), 13 bottom (Rich Kirchner), 21 bottom (David Woodfall), 25 bottom (Andy Rouse). Ecoscene: pages 1 & 23 top (Tom Ennis), 4 (Andrew D. R. Brown), 21 top (Sally Morgan), 25 top (Anthony Cooper). Panos Pictures: pages 23 bottom (Jean-Léo Dugast), 27 bottom (Arabella Cecil), 29 top (Fred Hoogervorst). Environmental Images: pages 24 (Clive Jones). Still Pictures: pages 5 top (Fritz Polking), 8 (Compost/Visage), 9 top (Mark Edwards), 11 (Kevin Schafer), 12 (Thomas D. Mangelsen), 15 top (Thomas Raupach), 26 (Roland Seitre), 27 bottom left (Jorgen Schytte), 29 top (Ray Pforiner). Science Photo Library: page 10 top right (Jeff Lepore). Bruce Coleman Ltd: pages 10 bottom left (Jane Burton), 15 bottom (Dr. Charles Henneghien), 22 John Cancalosi), 28 (Trevor Barrett).

Artwork: Raymond Turvey.

Franklin Watts is a division of Hachette Children's Books, an Hachette Livre UK company.

Note to parents and teachers: Every effort has been made by the publisher to ensure that websites listed are suitable for children, that they are of the highest educational value, and that they contain no inappropriate or offensive material. However, because of the nature of the Internet, it is impossible to guarantee that the contents of these sites will not be altered. We strongly advise that Internet access is supervised by a responsible adult.

CONTENTS

BIODIVERSITY

We know of over a million different species (kinds) of plants and animals. But there may be millions more that we do not know about. We call this variety of living things biodiversity.

Different homes

The place where an animal or plant lives is called its **habitat.** Different kinds of living things have different habitats. They are often **adapted** so that they can live easily in their habitat. For example, penguins are adapted to live in the cold Antarctic.

*This meadow is a habitat for many different **species** of plants and animals.*

Giant pandas mostly eat bamboo. If bamboo forests are cut down, they may starve.

On the Ground

In China, there are special forest **nature reserves** for pandas to live in.

Under threat

*These giraffe and **eland** live on the African grasslands. Many other species of animals live there.*

Wildlife is in danger. People use land for homes, farms and factories, so there is less space for wildlife. People also create **pollution**, which harms animals and plants. Some have died out completely. We say they have become **extinct**.

LIVING TOGETHER

Different plants and animals often live together in the same habitat.

Food chains

Some animals eat plants, and some eat other animals, which eat plants. This means that plants and animals are linked by what they eat. We call these links **food chains.** Some plants or animals are parts of several food chains. For example, both hyenas and lions eat zebras. Food chains that are linked together are called food webs.

If the lions in this food chain died, there would be too many zebras. They would eat too much grass and run out of food. Many would starve.

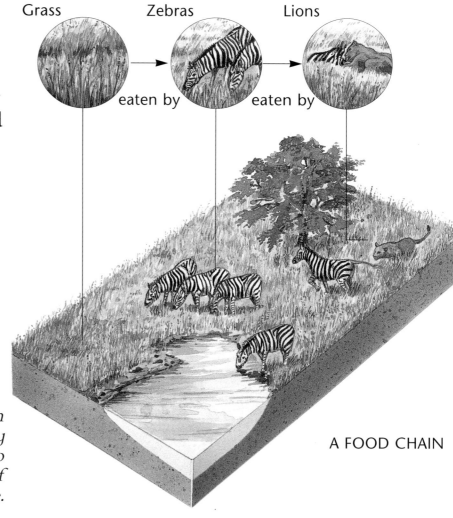

Grass   Zebras   Lions

eaten by   eaten by

A FOOD CHAIN

This bateleur eagle is part of many food chains. It eats eggs, snakes, insects and dead animals.

FOOD WEBS

Food webs are made up of many food chains. The grassland of Africa has a large food web. The links in each food chain start with the plant or animal being eaten.

Disappearing wildlife

It is important to make sure the different kinds of plants and animals on Earth do not die out. We call this **conserving** them. To do this, we need to conserve their habitats, too. Habitats sometimes disappear because of natural things. But, often, people damage the **environment**, so plants and animals cannot live in it. If they have nowhere to live, they die out. Saving wildlife is very difficult if its habitat disappears.

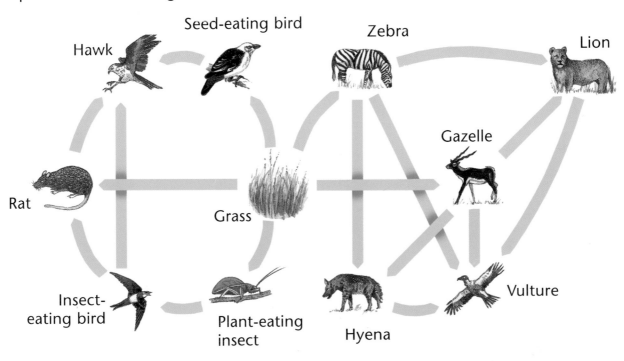

Hawk   Seed-eating bird   Zebra   Lion

Gazelle

Rat

Grass

Insect-eating bird   Plant-eating insect   Hyena   Vulture

RAINFOREST LIFE

Tropical rainforests are in warm, wet parts of the world. They cover nearly one-fifth of the Earth's surface. But two-thirds of all our wildlife lives there.

This is the biggest flower in the world. It is a rafflesia, from the rainforest of Indonesia.

Rich rainforests

In **tropical rainforests** there is more **biodiversity** than in any other habitat. Hundreds of different trees and birds, and thousands of different insects live there. Many creatures live high up in the forest trees. They eat leaves, nuts, and each other. Smaller animals live on the floor of the forest. So do **fungi**, and tiny living creatures called **bacteria**. These break down rotting plants.

This rainforest in Brazil was chopped down. When the trees disappeared, so did the animals.

This golden lion tamarin is a monkey from forests in Brazil, South America.

On the Ground

Forests where some monkeys live are disappearing. But there are reserves where they can live safely.

Saving forests

Half of all the rainforests have been chopped down. People want the wood, and they want the land for factories, farms and houses. But if the trees go, the animals have no homes. Now some people are trying to conserve the forests. They take only a few trees, and leave the rest.

NORTHERN FORESTS

Forests called boreal forests stretch across the northern part of the world. The trees are conifers (fir and pine trees), which can live through cold winters. Wolves, bears, squirrels and moose live there.

Wolves hunt in groups. There is not much food for them, so they must travel long distances.

Barn owls live in the cold forests of the north. They have nests in old, hollow trees.

Eco Thought

Wolves used to be common in Europe. But people killed most of them because they hunted farm animals.

Disappearing forests

Boreal forests used to be safe from people, because they were hard to reach. But now many have been chopped down for their wood. It is used to make furniture, matches and paper. Sometimes, large parts of the forest are chopped down to make space for oil wells and mines.

This pipeline in Alaska, North America, is carrying oil. The boreal forest is at risk from the oil industry.

Planting for the future

A lot of the forest in Europe and America has been chopped down. New trees, which grow fast, have been planted instead. This means there will always be plenty of wood, and we say the forest is **sustainable**. But these forests are not as good for wildlife as the older forests. In some places, the forest is cut down in small patches. New trees are planted, so there are trees of different ages. This is better for wildlife.

Try this
Study a big tree near your home. Look for different plants and animals living on it. There may be mosses and ferns, insects and other small animals.

11

FROZEN PLACES

The Arctic and Antarctic are the coldest places on Earth. In winter, it can be -60°C. There are fierce winds and no sunlight. In summer, it is hardly ever above 0°C.

Living in cold places

Only a few animals and plants are able to live in very cold places. Many, such as polar bears and **Arctic** foxes, have thick fur to keep them warm. Seals have a thick layer of fat called blubber under their skins, which also helps to keep them warm.

Polar bears live in the Arctic.

12

On the Ground

The biggest pollution incident in Alaska was when a shipwreck sent 50 million litres of oil into the sea there. This happened in 1989.

Tourists visiting the sea off Alaska.

Scientists on ice

Many scientists live and work in the Antarctic. They use **snowmobiles,** aircraft and food supplies. All these can bring pollution.

A plane brings in supplies for scientists working in the Antarctic.

Arctic tourists

Tourists like to visit the Arctic and Antarctic. But these environments are easy to harm. Rubbish will not rot, and plants take a long time to grow if they are damaged.

Digging deep

The rocks in icy places may contain oil, coal or metals. We need these, but getting them can harm the environment. In 1991, more than 40 countries agreed not to dig mines in the Antarctic for 50 years.

OPEN SEAS

Seas and oceans cover nearly two-thirds of the Earth. There are many different habitats under the water, and they all have their own plants and animals.

Coral reefs

Coral reefs lie underwater near the shore, in warm and cold seas. They are made up of the skeletons of tiny animals called corals. Around one-quarter of all the animals in the sea live among coral reefs.

Reefs under threat

Many things can damage coral reefs. Pollution can kill the creatures that live there, and break the food chains. Divers may catch colourful fish to sell for aquariums. Sometimes, people blow up coral to use it for building. Boats can damage coral, too.

Divers sometimes break off coral to sell to tourists, and this can harm reefs.

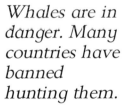

Fishermen pull in the nets, which are full of fish.

Overfishing

People catch fish and shellfish to eat. But there are many more people than in the past, and new ways of fishing. We are catching too many fish. We are not leaving enough to breed and make new fish. Some species may die out soon.

Saving sea-life

Many countries now try to make sure that fishermen do not catch too many fish. They must use nets with large holes, which let small, young fish escape. But the wildlife in our oceans is also in danger from pollution.

Whales are in danger. Many countries have banned hunting them.

On the Ground

People can make artificial coral reefs. They put objects such as old cars under water. Coral grows over them.

RIVERS AND PONDS

There are always plenty of plants and animals in a healthy river. But pollution damages everything that lives there.

Polluting the water

There are many towns close to rivers. Waste from factories and homes flows into the rivers, and the pollution spreads all along the river.

Harming wildlife

Fish, shellfish, frogs and toads suffer first from pollution. So do the birds that feed on them. In the end, only the strongest plants and animals can survive.

CLEAN AND POLLUTED RIVERS

Clean river

Many shellfish, fish, birds and insects can live in a river if the water is clean. Plants grow along its banks. If there is pollution in the water, there may only be worms and a few kinds of fish. Green **algae** makes the water dark.

Polluted river

Oxygen

The **fertilizers** that farmers use have chemicals in them that help plants grow. If they get into water, they make tiny plants called algae grow very fast. These cut out the light that other plants need. Also, living things called bacteria break down the algae. This uses up the gas oxygen, which water animals need. Many die and the whole food chain is harmed.

This is a water scorpion. It hunts small fish and tadpoles. It needs clean water.

Try this

With an adult, catch some river animals in a net. Keep them wet. Make a note of what they are and put them back in the water.

Many animals live in ponds. Some, such as freshwater shrimps, only live in clean water.

FARMS

There are more people in the world, so we need to grow more food. There are farms on land where wildlife used to live.

Wildlife deserts

Today, farmers grow crops on land that was once grassland. Wild animals can no longer live there. This has happened in North America and Russia. For wildlife, this farmland is like a desert.

Killing the pests

Farmers use chemicals called pesticides to kill insects that damage crops. These can harm other wild creatures, such as the birds that eat insects.

Machines help farmers. But they can harm wildlife, such as field mice.

Eco Thought
Some farming helps wildlife. Sheep help keep grass clear of trees, so other grassland animals can share the grass.

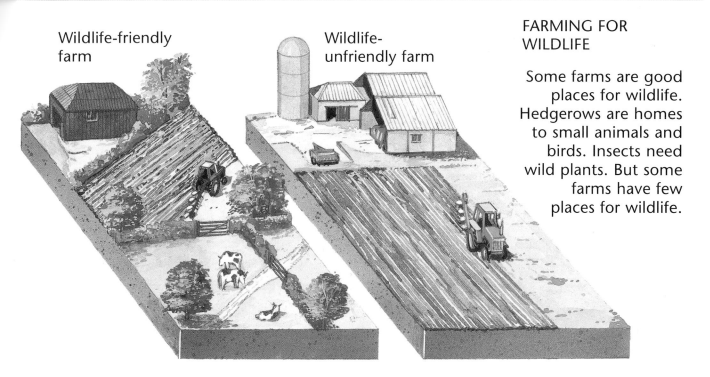

Wildlife-friendly farm

Wildlife-unfriendly farm

Some farms are good places for wildlife. Hedgerows are homes to small animals and birds. Insects need wild plants. But some farms have few places for wildlife.

Friendly farms

Farmers can grow crops and look after wildlife at the same time. They can leave corners of fields for wild plants and animals. They can plant trees, dig ponds and plant hedgerows. They may find that there are animals that will eat pests, so there is no need for pesticides.

Trees grow in these rice fields in Bali, in Indonesia.

GREEN CITIES

Towns and cities are getting bigger. There is less countryside for wildlife. But some plants and animals have learned to live in parks and gardens.

Storks nesting on the top of a church.

New homes

Some birds like to nest on cliffs, but they will also nest on high buildings. In some cities, people build special nesting places for birds on buildings. Other animals, such as snails or lizards live in holes in walls. Animals make their homes in parks and in the trees that grow along roads. Ponds, rivers and canals are also home to wildlife. Insects feed off the plants in gardens.

Try this

Plant flowers with strong scents in a window box or a tub. These plants may attract birds and insects.

Urban pests

Many animals that live in cities are pests, such as rats and mice. They live in old buildings, drains and sewers. They eat rubbish, and carry diseases. In cities in hot countries there are insects called termites that eat wooden houses.

Parks in cities can be home to many wild animals.

There was once a coal mine on this land. Now the mine has gone, and people have planted trees here instead.

Unused land

There are often places in cities where there were once factories or old buildings. Many plants, birds and butterflies can live there. Sometimes these places are turned into nature reserves. But often they are used for new buildings instead.

HUNTING

Long ago, nearly all people hunted animals for meat to eat and fur for clothes. Today, people still hunt animals, but few of them really need to.

On the Ground

In Africa, poachers kill rhinos for their horns. Sometimes people take off the horns, so poachers will not harm the rhinos.

Ivory and horn

It is against the law to hunt some animals. Illegal hunting is called poaching. **Poachers** kill elephants for their tusks, which are called **ivory.** They kill rhinos for their horns. There are now more elephants than there were, and some countries want to allow hunting again.

These goods were all made from animals that were hunted illegally.

Fur coats

Many rare animals are hunted illegally. These include leopards, tigers and lynxes. Hunters still kill these, so their skins can be made into fur coats. The hunters also kill snakes and crocodiles, to make bags and shoes.

These rare creatures were on sale in a market in Peru, South America

Orchids usually grow in rainforests. These were grown in greenhouses.

Collecting plants

Some people collect rare plants. They take them from wild places and sell them to people who want them in their gardens.

Stopping the trade

More than 150 countries have joined a group called CITES (Convention on International Trade in **Endangered** Species). It was set up in 1975. It bans hunting and selling rare plants and animals.

Try this
Don't pick wild flowers or take plants from wild places.

SAVING WILDLIFE

Many species of animals are in danger of becoming extinct. We must find ways to save them.

Scientists have given this lion an injection to make it sleep. They can then check to see how healthy it is.

Learning

If scientists want to save animals, they need to know where they live and what they eat. They need to know which animals hunt them. To save plants, they must learn about where and how they grow.

Numbers

Wild animals die out if there are too few of them. There must be enough for them to find mates and breed. To be safe, there needs to be 300 to 500 of a species.

On the Ground

There are only about 400 Siberian tigers left in the wild. However, around 400 more have been bred in zoos. Maybe, one day, more can be set free.

Parks for animals

In some places, there are national parks, where people live with animals but do not hunt them. Sometimes, animals that are in danger are moved to safer places, or to wildlife parks or zoos.

White rhino are in danger of dying out. Here, they are safe in a wildlife park.

Elephants in a national park. Here, they are safer from poachers.

Captive breeding

When animals are bred in zoos, this is called **captive breeding.** It does not work for all animals. Often, it is better to keep groups of the animals in safe areas, and let them breed there. Later, some can be set free to live as wild animals.

On the Ground

The last species of wild horse is Przewalski's horse, from Mongolia. It died out in the wild. But some were bred in zoos, and taken back to Mongolia and set free.

RESCUE PLANS

Sometimes there are very few of an animal or plant left. Scientists must plan carefully in order to save them.

A variety of animals

If there are large numbers of a kind of animal, there is a lot of variety. If there are just a few, there is not much variety. They may be different sizes, or colours. When scientists breed animals in captivity, they try to keep this variety. It is not good to breed animals that are close relations, as these may be weak.

Eco Thought

Ten per cent of the different kinds of trees in the world are in danger. One-quarter are protected by law.

These students are holding rare scarlet macaws. Each young bird is at a different stage in its life.

Animal exchange

Zoos keep records of the parents of their animals. They check that animals do not mate with close relations. Zoos sometimes borrow animals from each other, so they can breed from them. Pandas are often exchanged like this.

This tiger was bred in captivity. Then it was set free in a national park.

Scientists in a seed bank. They look for the best seeds to breed new plants from.

Seed banks

It is important not to let any plants die out. They may be useful one day as crops, or to make medicines. So scientists grow large numbers of different plants in botanical gardens. They also keep collections of seeds, called **seed banks.** They check these every few years, to see if they can still grow into plants. Sometimes they use the seeds to grow new plants, to make more seeds.

WHAT CAN WE DO?

People and governments can work together to make our world safer for wild animals and plants.

These children in South Africa are learning about local wild plants and animals.

Try this

Local wildlife groups often need people to help out. Join a local group and do jobs like planting trees and making nest boxes.

Taking action

In 2002, there was a meeting called the World Summit on Sustainable Development. Governments from around the world agreed to protect biodiversity. They agreed to try to stop species being lost, and to improve the environment. They have set up parks, and made laws to stop people catching, killing or selling species that are in danger.

Clearing up rubbish on a beach in the United States.

On the Ground

The World Wildlife Fund is one of the biggest wildlife organizations in the world. It has over 5,000,000 supporters.

These marks warn drivers that badgers cross this road.

Local wildlife

We can help bring wild animals close to our homes and schools. One way is to make a bird table and put food onto it. Put out nuts, seeds, fat and stale bread. You can also put up nesting boxes, where birds such as blue tits can lay their eggs and look after their young. At school, you can make a wildlife corner, with wild plants and a small pond.

Watching wildlife

You can learn about animals by watching them. Look for them in gardens, nature reserves and parks. You can also join organizations that help conserve wildlife.

FACT FILE

Rare cat

The Iberian lynx lives in Spain and Portugal. There are almost none left, but now there are reserves for them.

The ibex

The Himalayan ibex is a wild goat from Pakistan. It was in danger of dying out, but WWF helped local people look after the ibex's habitat. Now there are over 1,000 ibex.

Coral

There is a huge coral reef off the coast of Australia. It is called the Great Barrier Reef, and it is the biggest marine (sea) national park in the world. To keep it safe, habitats nearby are protected as well.

Polluted lake

Lake Baikal, in Russia is 1,485 metres deep. It is the deepest lake in the world. There are many animals that live only in this lake. One of these is a rare kind of seal. But Lake Baikal is polluted, and animals are hunted, so all these rare animals are in danger.

Seed banks

Scientists think there are 250,000 species of plants in the world. Only 6,000 are in seed banks. Kew Gardens, in London is the biggest seed bank in the world. Scientists there want to have 24,000 different kinds of seeds by 2010.

Websites

www.kidsplanet.org

www.yptenc.org.uk

www.rarespecies.org/kids/

www.nwf.org/kids

www.edenproject.com/

GLOSSARY

Adapted The way an animal or plant is made so that it can live easily in its environment.

Algae Tiny plants that live in the water.

Antarctic The far south of the Earth.

Arctic The far north of the Earth.

Bacteria Very tiny living things that are made up of just a single cell.

Boreal forests Forests in the far north, mainly made up of a kind of trees called conifers.

Captive breeding Letting animals breed while they are in captivity, e.g. in a zoo.

Conifers Trees such as fir trees or pine trees which keep their leaves all year round.

Conserve To protect.

Eland A kind of animal that lives in Africa. It eats grass.

Endangered In danger of becoming extinct.

Environment Things in our surroundings, including animals, plants, water and air.

Extinct When an animal or plant has died out, it is extinct.

Fertilizers Substances farmers add to the soil to help their crops grow.

Food chain The way living things are linked together by what eats them. For example, grass is eaten by zebras, which are eaten by lions.

Fungi Tiny living things that make mushrooms and toadstools.

Habitat Where a plant or animal lives.

Ivory The hard white material that elephants' tusks are made of.

Nature reserve A large area of land where wild animals and plants can live safely.

Pesticides Chemicals that will kill the insect pests that damage crops, such as greenfly.

Poachers People who hunt and kill animals that are protected.

Pollution Poisons in the environment.

Rainforests Thick forests that grow in warm, wet parts of the world.

Seed bank A store of seeds.

Snowmobile A sort of motorbike that is designed to travel on snow.

Species A kind of plant or animal.

Sustainable A forest that can survive, even when the wood from it is used.

Tropical Warm, wet parts of the world.

Wildlife Wild plants and animals.

INDEX